P9-EFG-701

The Universe

Revised Edition

Alvin Silverstein, Virginia Silverstein, and Laura Silverstein Nunn

Twenty-First Century Books
Minneapolis

Twenty-First Century Books
A division of Lerner Publishing Group, Inc.
241 First Avenue North
Minneapolis, MN 55401 U.S.A.

Website address: www.lernerbooks.com

Library of Congress Cataloging-in-Publication Data

Silverstein, Alvin.
     The universe / by Alvin & Virginia Silverstein & Laura Silverstein Nunn. —
   Rev. ed.
        p.   cm. — (Science concepts. Second series)
     Includes bibliographical references and index.
     ISBN 978-0-7613-3937-3 (lib. bdg. : alk. paper)
     1. Astronomy—Juvenile literature. 2. Solar system—Juvenilie literature.
   I. Silverstein, Virginia B. II. Nunn, Laura Silverstein. III. Title.
   QB46.S53 2009
   520—dc22   2007052245

Manufactured in the United States of America
1 2 3 4 5 6 – DP – 14 13 12 11 10 09

Contents

chapter one

Our Vast Universe

What's the first thing that comes to mind when you hear the word *universe*? If you're like most people, you think of the universe as big or huge. In fact, many people even use the word *universe* in everyday speech to refer to something that is bigger than you could possibly imagine. Actually, nobody knows how big the universe really is. But scientists define it as everything that exists. So everything in space—the Sun, the planets and their moons, and the countless stars—are all part of the universe.

To us, planet Earth seems like an enormous place. It is a world filled with miles and miles of land and oceans—so many places that you're not likely to see them all in a lifetime. What you may not realize, however, is that Earth is an extremely small part of the universe. Imagine an ant trying to travel over every inch of planet Earth. The ant is just a tiny speck compared to our planet. And yet, our Earth is an even smaller speck when compared to the whole universe.

When you look up at the sky, you can see countless stars in our universe.

How Did It All Begin?

Astronomers believe that the universe began about 13 to 15 billion years ago. There are many different theories about how it came into existence, but the most popular one is the big bang theory. The story goes that in the beginning, there was nothing—no matter, no light, and no energy.

At some point, a hot tiny speck of energy appeared. It was so hot and condensed that eventually it burst, and energy expanded outward. Matter started to form from the energy, which was mainly high-energy gamma radiation. Tiny particles of matter mixed with the energy like peas in hot soup. This was the start of our universe. Time and space began when the universe started to expand. The twentieth-century scientist Albert Einstein described the close link between space and time as the space-time continuum. He explained that once time existed, space could expand, which then allowed time to flow.

Soon the hot little universe started to cool. The gamma radiation lost some of its energy and turned into X-rays, light, and finally heat radiation. Particles of matter combined to form atoms, the basic building blocks of the chemical elements. At first only the simplest, lightest atoms were formed—those of hydrogen and helium.

In this early universe, matter was spread out in a thin fog of gases. The atoms pulled on one another, and after millions of years, they formed clouds suspended in clear, empty space. These clouds of gases were the beginnings of the

This illustration shows the big bang theory as a bright point of energy expanding outward.

galaxies (groups of stars) that exist today. Atoms joined to produce heavier elements and came together to form stars and planets. Our Sun was formed about 5 billion years ago, and planet Earth was formed about half a billion years later.

Scientists believe that life first appeared on Earth about three or four billion years ago. The first living things were simple organisms. Over time, they changed and developed—evolved—into more complex organisms that were better adapted to survive in their environment. Billions of years of evolution transformed these early creatures into the many diverse living things of our modern world.

Even today, the universe is still expanding. Scientists know this because when they look through powerful telescopes, they can see that the stars and other cosmic objects are moving away from one another farther into outer space. They are not sure whether the universe will go on expanding forever. Some scientists think that at some point, the universe will begin to contract (shrink). Eventually, it will reach a tiny point—a sort of reverse big bang. These two competing theories are called the open universe (expanding) and the closed universe (contracting). In the open universe theory, the stars would eventually burn out. The closed universe theory says that in the end, as the universe contracts, galaxies will join and the temperature will rise. Finally, in a "big crunch," all matter will disappear into a single "black hole." Will that be the end of everything? Some scientists think so, but others say that another big bang will start the process all over again.

Changing Views

For a very long time, people have been fascinated by the sky. They have watched the movements of the Sun and Moon and noticed the twinkling points of light in the night sky. They have learned to predict the changes in the sky that occur regularly throughout the year. Stonehenge, a circle of huge stones in Great Britain that dates back four thousand years, was apparently a tool for early astronomers.

How Big?

Earth (diameter)	about 8,000 miles (close to 13,000 kilometers)
Sun (diameter)	about 865,000 miles (about 1.4 million km)
Distance between Earth and Sun	93 million miles (150 million km)
Milky Way galaxy (diameter)	600,000 trillion miles (1 million trillion km)
Observable universe (diameter)	more than 150 billion trillion miles (more than 250 billion trillion km)

Earth may seem huge to us, but when compared to the size of the Sun, it is quite small.

The arrangement of stones at Stonehenge in England allowed ancient astronomers to track the seasons, observing key dates such as the first day of summer. That is when the Sun reaches its highest point in the sky. With more hours of daylight than any other date, it is the longest day of the year.

Standing at the center of the circle, a person would see the Sun rise over different stones at different times of the year.

Ancient astronomers did not realize how big the universe was. They thought that it consisted of only what they could see—Earth, Sun, Moon, planets, and stars. They considered the sky a kind of ceiling with lights suspended from it. For thousands of years, most people believed that Earth was the center of the universe and the other planets and the Sun all traveled around Earth. In the early 1500s, a Polish astronomer, Nicolaus Copernicus, challenged these views. He believed that Earth was like the other planets and that they all moved around the Sun. Many people refused to believe Copernicus's ideas at the time.

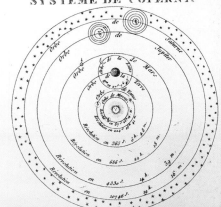

SYSTEME DE COPERNIC

Copernic, aussi instruit que sage, replace le soleil immobile au centre du monde, comme un flambeau qui l'éclaire et le vivifie; il lui donne un mouvement de rotation sur lui même. Dans son système, le mouvement diurne de tout le ciel s'explique avec une extrème facilité; il suffit en effet que l'habitant de la terre tourne autour de l'axe, d'occident en orient, pour que tous les astres lui paroissent rouler d'orient en occident et qu'il rapporte au soleil le mouvement qui n'est réel que pour la terre. Mais tandis que la terre tourne sur elle même en 24 heures, elle décrit une orbite autour du soleil, dans l'espace d'une année. Par ce mouvement propre, que l'illusion attribue au soleil, cet astre semble s'avancer chaque jour d'environ un degré vers l'orient, pendant qu'il est emporté chaque jour avec tout le ciel d'un mouvement commun vers l'occident. La trace de ce mouvement annuel est l'écliptique, au bout de 365 jours, une étoile observée se reconnoît à la même heure, au même lieu, où elle s'étoit montrée l'année précédente, à pareil jour.

Above: *This painting of Nicolaus Copernicus shows the Polish astronomer working on his diagram of a sun-centered solar system (right). Copernicus came up with his views on the universe in the early 1500s.*

It wasn't until a century later that Copernicus's theory was proven correct by an Italian astronomer, Galileo Galilei. In 1609 Galileo became the first person to use a telescope to look at the sky. For the first time, scientists could see planets and their moons up close. Galileo recorded all his discoveries. For instance, when he looked up at Jupiter, he saw four tiny stars close by. He realized these must be moons of Jupiter because he was able to track their orbits around the planet. In 1632 Galileo published his findings, which supported Copernicus's ideas

This painting from 1633 shows Galileo Galilei on trial in front of clergy in the Roman Catholic Church. Members of the church did not want Galileo to teach his controversial views on the universe.

that all the planets, including Earth, move around the Sun. This discovery angered many important people in the Roman Catholic Church, who considered the idea false and absurd. As a result, Galileo spent the rest of his life under house arrest. Eventually, people came to accept that the planets and their moons do, indeed, move around the Sun.

Scientists continued to use and develop powerful telescopes

Did You Know?

In 1992, more than 350 years after Galileo's discoveries, the Catholic Church finally released a statement acknowledging that Earth moves around the Sun.

and other devices to view great distances into space. New, modern technologies have made it possible for humans to explore space and make journeys that once seemed impossible. Space probes sent into outer space have sent back never-before-seen pictures of the planets, stars, and other objects beyond our solar system. Thanks to these continuing efforts, new discoveries are constantly being made. Yet there is still so much to learn about our vast universe.

Our Solar System

If you wake up early on a sunny morning, you will see the Sun slowly rising in the east. By lunchtime, the Sun appears to be high in the sky, shining brightly. Around dinnertime, the Sun is low in the western sky, ready to disappear below the horizon and call it a day. As you follow the Sun throughout the day—from morning to afternoon to evening—you may think the Sun has moved across the sky. So you can see why people used to think that the Sun traveled around Earth.

From sunrise to sunset, it is easy to see why people used to believe the Sun traveled around Earth, instead of the other way around.

Of course, the Sun does not move around our planet. The Sun looks as if it is moving across the sky because Earth is actually rotating, turning on its axis. Different parts of the globe are directly facing the Sun at different times of the day. One complete rotation takes one day (twenty-four hours).

Another kind of movement occurs, as well. Earth is moving around the Sun in a path called an orbit. This path has the form of an ellipse (oval). A complete trip around Earth's orbit, a revolution, takes one year (about 365 days). Actually, Earth is just one of eight planets that orbit our star, the Sun. The Sun, eight planets, and a collection of asteroids, comets, and moons make up the solar system.

Earth moves around the Sun in an elliptical orbit (like a flattened circle). A complete trip takes about 365 days. On the autumnal and vernal (spring) equinoxes, the periods of daylight and darkness are exactly the same. On the winter solstice, Earth has its shortest day length. Its day length is longest on the summer solstice.

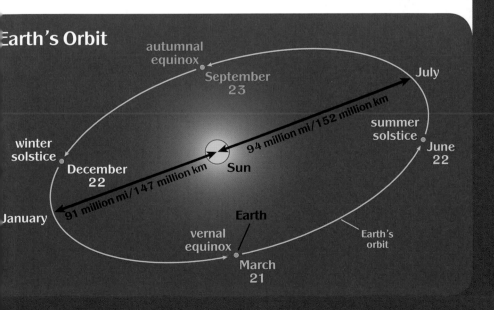

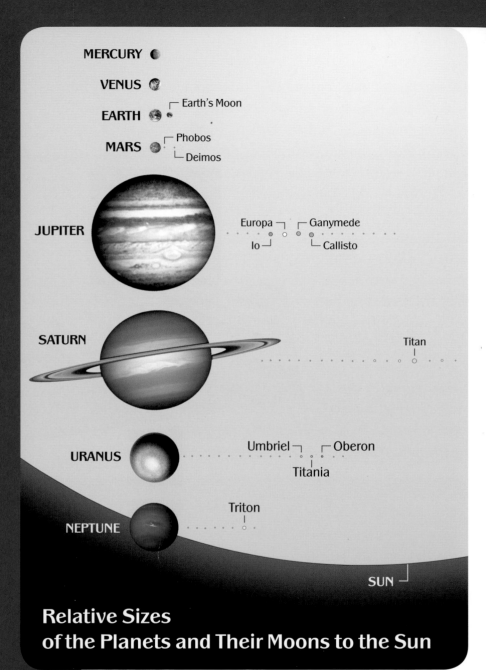

MERCURY

VENUS

EARTH — Earth's Moon

MARS — Phobos
— Deimos

JUPITER — Europa — Ganymede
Io — — Callisto

SATURN — Titan

URANUS — Umbriel — Oberon
Titania

NEPTUNE — Triton

SUN

Relative Sizes
of the Planets and Their Moons to the Sun

This image shows the planets and moons of our solar system, shown to the scale of the Sun.

In order, going outward from the Sun, the planets in our solar system are Mercury, Venus, Earth, Mars, Jupiter, Saturn, Uranus, and Neptune.

Mutual Attraction

Our solar system is located in a spiral-shaped mass called the Milky Way galaxy. The Milky Way is a huge collection of dust, gas, and stars. The Sun is actually only one of billions of stars in the Milky Way. And the Milky Way is only one of countless galaxies in the universe.

> Did You Know?
> Earth moves in its orbit around the Sun at an average speed of 66,600 miles (107,200 km) an hour. We don't notice the movement because we are moving right along with it.

Everything in the Milky Way is controlled by gravity. Gravity is a force that holds the Sun, the planets, and the stars together. Gravity also keeps the planets in their orbits around the Sun and the moons in orbits around the planets. The motion of these bodies would send them flying off into space if it were not for the inward pull of gravity. Have you ever swung a ball on a string in a circle around you? If the string breaks, the ball's movement sends it flying off. The pull of the string toward you is like the attractive force of gravity.

Gravity helps to determine the movements of the stars and galaxies as well. The Sun and all the other stars in the entire Milky Way are orbiting the center of the galaxy, in much the same way the planets of the solar system orbit the Sun. It takes the Sun about 250 million years to complete one circular trip in its orbit around the center of the galaxy. The galaxies are

Our solar system is located in the Milky Way galaxy, which spins around like a giant pinwheel, as shown in this illustration.

Did You Know?

The Sun is the closest star to us—about 93 million miles (150 million km) away!

also moving, as their gravity acts on nearby galaxies.

The strength of the mutual attraction between the Sun and each planet is determined both by the size of the two objects pulling on each other and by the distance between them. Larger objects have a greater pull, but the strength of gravity decreases very rapidly as the distance increases. The planets' movements are also affected by the attraction of the other planets. These effects of gravity are much smaller than the attraction of the Sun (because the planets are so much smaller than the Sun). But they are enough to make slight changes in the planets' orbits. In fact, some of the outer planets in our solar system were discovered after astronomers realized that the movements of the inner planets did not quite match the orbits calculated for them. From disturbances of the orbits, astronomers figured that there must be another planet-sized body farther out that was pulling on them.

How Much Do You Weigh?

The Sun's large size gives it a much greater gravitational pull than that of any of the planets. So a person who weighs 100 pounds (45 kilograms) on Earth would weigh 2,800 pounds (1,270 kg) on the Sun.

The Sun

The Sun is the center of our solar system. For a star, the Sun isn't very big—it's just medium size. But compared to the planets that orbit it, the Sun is enormous. In fact, the Sun's mass (weight) is 745 times greater than that of all the planets in the solar system combined.

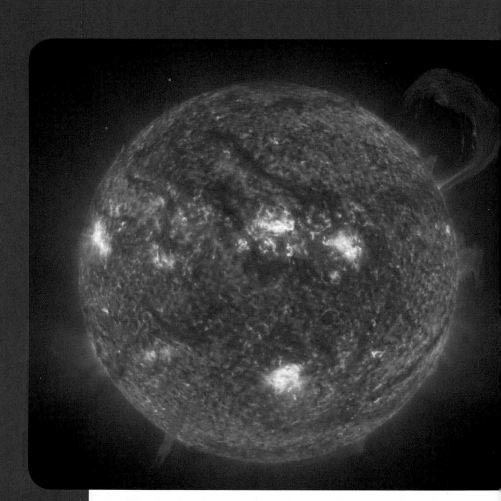

The Sun is a burning ball of gas that does not have a solid surface.

The Sun is not solid, like Earth. The Sun is a fiery hot ball of gas. It is constantly moving, rotating around its axis about once every twenty-seven days. But the gases that make up the Sun do not all move together: the gases at the equator move faster than those at the poles at the ends of the axis.

The Sun's energy is created inside its core (center). This is where nuclear reactions take place. Enormous amounts of energy are released. The energy gradually moves out to the Sun's surface, called the photosphere. Solar energy from the core can take up to 10 million years to reach the surface of the Sun. From the photosphere, energy travels outward into space, mostly in the form of light and infrared radiation (heat). The energy in the sunlight that's streaming over you on a bright sunny day actually formed millions of years ago.

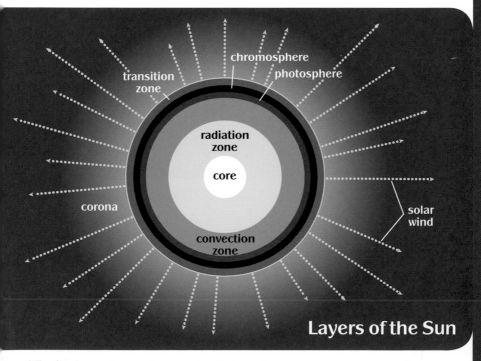

Layers of the Sun

The Sun's core is a nuclear reactor that produces enormous amounts of energy. This energy radiates outward and is carried by currents of moving gases to the outer layers. Light and heat then travel outward into space. Some of this solar energy reaches Earth's surface.

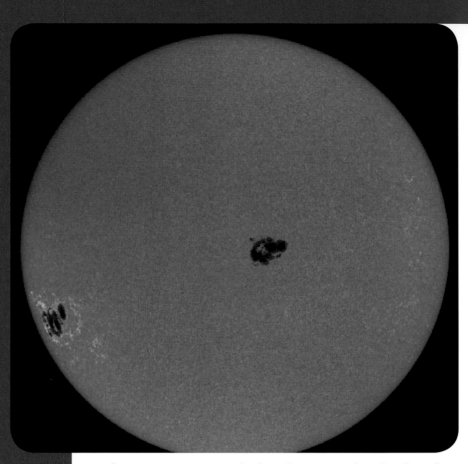

Sunspots are areas on the Sun that are much cooler than the surrounding areas.

The Sun is a giant magnet, with magnetic field lines that run between its north and south poles. The different speeds of movement of the gases pull and stretch the magnetic field lines, twisting them. Sometimes loops of magnetism break through to the surface, forming sunspots. These are dark spots that range from a few hundred miles up to 50,000 miles (80,000 km) across. They look dark because the magnetic fields prevent hot gases from rising to the surface.

Hot Stuff

The Sun's core is estimated to have a temperature of 27 million°F (15 million°C). The temperature on the Sun's surface reaches as much as 9,900°F (5,500°C). Hot, electrically charged gas particles constantly escape from the Sun's surface and fly out into space. The flow of charged particles forms the solar wind, which travels rapidly. Its speed is as high as 470 miles (750 km) per second by the time it reaches Earth.

Occasionally, some of the Sun's stored energy is released from the surface in a dramatic burst called a solar flare. The temperature of the solar flare is about twice as high as the temperature of the Sun's surface. Heat, light, and fast-moving atomic particles splash out into space. Its effects can be felt on Earth, where the radiation disrupts radio signals.

This image shows a solar flare splashing out into space from the Sun's surface.

So these areas are much cooler than the rest of the Sun. The interaction of the Sun's magnetism and its uneven rotation can also produce violent eruptions called solar flares. They release hot gases from below the surface.

The Sun showers light and heat energy on all the planets in the solar system. In addition to the visible light, the Sun's radiation also includes radio waves, ultraviolet rays, and X-rays. Ultraviolet rays can cause sunburn and skin cancer. X-rays can damage tissues. Fortunately, Earth's atmosphere shields us from most of the damaging solar radiation.

The Moon is seen setting behind a thin layer of Earth's atmosphere in this photo taken from the orbiting space shuttle Columbia. *The atmosphere is very important in keeping most of the Sun's radiation from Earth.*

The amount of solar energy the planets receive depends on their distance from the Sun. For instance, Mercury, the planet closest to the Sun, receives the most sunlight. Neptune is the farthest planet from the Sun and receives the least.

On Earth the Sun's energy is important to the survival of all living things—people, animals, and plants. Plants use the sunlight to turn water, carbon dioxide, and other raw materials into food. This food is used by the plants and also by the animals that feed on them.

chapter three

The Planets

After the Sun, the largest members of the solar system are the planets. Scientists have split the eight planets into two main groups according to their location. The inner planets include the first four planets—Mercury, Venus, Earth, and Mars. The outer planets include the next four—Jupiter, Saturn, Uranus, and Neptune.

What Happened to Pluto?

For years, schoolchildren learned all about the nine planets in our solar system, from Mercury to Pluto. But in 2006, the International Astronomical Union (IAU), a committee of astronomers, announced that Pluto would no longer be considered a planet. Astronomers had been arguing about whether or not Pluto is a planet for a long time. But for the rest of the world, this news was shocking.

Pluto had been a "real planet" for seventy-six years. Since 2006 it has been classified as a dwarf planet. So why the change after all these years? In 2006

This illustration shows the planets lined up in order to the right of the Sun.
Left to right: *The Sun, Mercury, Venus, Earth, Mars, Jupiter, Saturn,*
Uranus, and Neptune are shown surrounded by other stars in the universe.

the IAU clearly defined a planet for the first time—and Pluto
did not fit the description. The IAU states that a planet must
meet three conditions: A planet must orbit the Sun. It has
to be big enough for its own gravity to squish it into a round
shape. And finally, it must have its own orbit with no other
bodies in its path. Pluto follows an irregular orbit around the
Sun, crossing Neptune's path. Therefore, it does not follow
the third rule.

Even though current schoolbooks talk about the *eight* planets
in our solar system, Pluto's status continues to be a hot topic.

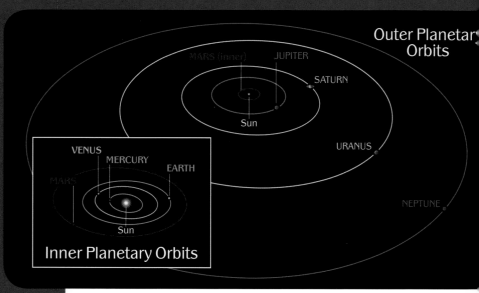

MARS (inner)   JUPITER

SATURN

Sun

URANUS

VENUS

MERCURY

EARTH

MARS

Sun

NEPTUNE

Inner Planetary Orbits

The orbits of all the planets in the solar system are shown here. The orbits of the inner planets are depicted in a blown-up box because they are so much smaller than the orbits of the outer planets when drawn to scale.

The planets of our solar system are separated into two groups to emphasize some important differences. For instance, the inner planets are much smaller than the outer planet "giants." Also, the inner planets are made mostly of rock and are sometimes known as the rock or terrestrial (Earth-like) planets. The four outer planets—Jupiter, Saturn, Uranus, and Neptune— are known as gas giants because they are mostly hydrogen and helium in gas and liquid form.

The Planets in Our Solar System

Mercury: Mercury is the closest planet to the Sun. (To someone on Mercury, the Sun would look about three times as big as it does from Earth.) Temperatures on this planet can go to extremes—hot enough to melt metal during the day and frigid at night. That's because Mercury has practically no atmosphere to trap the Sun's heat and warm the planet. Without an atmosphere to scatter light rays, Mercury's sky is dark even during the day. Also, without an atmosphere to carry sound waves, astronauts on Mercury would have to use a radio transmitter to talk to one another.

Venus: Venus is sometimes called Earth's twin because it is similar to our planet in size and weight. Like Earth, Venus has an atmosphere, but that's all they have in common. Venus is surrounded by a thick layer of clouds made of a poisonous gas, sulfuric acid. The atmospheric pressure on Venus is also much stronger than it is on Earth. Its atmosphere consists mostly of carbon dioxide, which is much heavier than the oxygen and nitrogen in Earth's atmosphere. In fact, you would be squashed if you stood on Venus.

Venus is the hottest planet in the solar system. The carbon dioxide in its atmosphere acts like a blanket to hold in the heat radiated by the Sun. Scientists call this the greenhouse effect, because

NASA (National Aeronautics and Space Administration) pieced together a combination of photos to create this full image of Venus's surface. The bright band across the middle is Aphrodite Terra, an area similar to the continents on Earth.

the atmosphere traps heat, warming the planet's surface, much as the glass walls of a greenhouse trap heat. The surface temperature stays burning hot, even at night.

Venus looks brighter than any planets or stars, except our Sun. That's because the Sun's rays are reflected (bounced back) when they hit Venus's thick clouds.

Earth: Earth is the only planet in the solar system that can support life (as far as we know). It is surrounded by an atmosphere that contains oxygen, a gas almost all living things need to live. Plants and animals can live just about anywhere on Earth's surface because our planet is just the right distance from the Sun. Temperatures can vary greatly on Earth, but they do not get too hot or too cold for living things to survive. Earth is the only planet where water can exist in both liquid and solid (ice) forms.

Like the Sun and most of the other planets, Earth is like a huge magnet. It has a strong magnetic field that covers the areas surrounding the North Pole and the South Pole. We can find our way around Earth's surface using a magnetic compass because of the magnetic field. Earth's magnetic field actually protects the planet from the effects of the solar wind. Charged particles that fly toward Earth are caught in Earth's magnetic field. They form two doughnut-shaped regions of high-energy radiation thousands of miles above Earth's surface. Astronomers call these regions the Van Allen belts. Astronauts on flights from Earth to the Moon must fly through the Van Allen belts. Special shielding on the outside of the spacecraft protects them from the dangerous radiations.

Earth is sometimes called the "blue planet" because most of its surface—about 70 percent—is made up of water, mostly oceans. From space, Earth looks like a giant blue marble with swirls of green, brown, and white. The white clouds that surround the planet are made of water vapor.

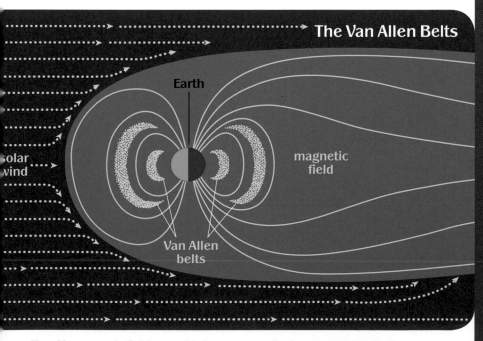

Earth's magnetic field traps high-energy radiations streaming in from the Sun in two doughnut-shaped regions called the Van Allen belts. They shield Earth from radiations that could damage living things.

Planet	Average Distance from the Sun	Rotation (day)
MERCURY	36 million miles (58 million km)	59 Earth days
VENUS	67 million miles (108 million km)	243 Earth days
EARTH	93 million miles (150 million km)	23 hrs. 56 min.
MARS	142 million miles (228 million km)	24 hrs. 37 min.
JUPITER	484 million miles (779 million km)	10 hrs.
SATURN	888 million miles (1.43 billion km)	10 hrs. 39 min.
URANUS	1.78 billion miles (2.86 billion km)	17 hrs.
NEPTUNE	2.79 billion miles (4.49 billion km)	16 hrs.

Revolution (year)	Diameter Mass	Average Temperature	Number of Moons/Rings
88 Earth days	3,031 miles (4,878 km) 2/5 Earth mass	−300°F (−185°C) to 800°F (427°C)	None/none
225 Earth days	7,520 miles (12,100 km) 4/5 Earth mass	About 900°F (500°C) surface	None/none
365.24 days	7,926 miles (12,756 km) 1 Earth mass	About 57°F (14°C) surface	1/none
687 Earth days	4,217 miles (6,787 km) 1/10 Earth mass	−81°F (−63°C) surface	2/none
12 Earth years	86,885 miles (139,828 km) 318 Earth mass	−243°F (−153°C) at cloud tops	63/4
29 Earth years	72,371 miles (116,470 km) 95 Earth mass	−300°F (−185°C) at cloud tops	60+/7 major rings
84 Earth years	31,520 miles (50,727 km) 14.5 Earth mass	−353°F (−214°C)	27/11
164 Earth years	30,775 miles (49,528 km) 17.1 Earth mass	−373°F (−225°C)	13/4

The water vapor comes from the surface of oceans, lakes, and rivers, where some of the liquid water turns into gas. Clouds produce rain, snow, sleet, and hail. The Sun's heat energy sets Earth's atmosphere constantly moving and churning, which causes a variety of weather conditions.

The brightest object in Earth's night sky is its Moon. The Moon appears so bright because its surface reflects sunlight. Unlike Earth, the Moon does not have an atmosphere and cannot support life. Temperatures on the Moon go to extremes—from a sweltering 240°F

This photo shows the Moon in the night sky with stars all around.

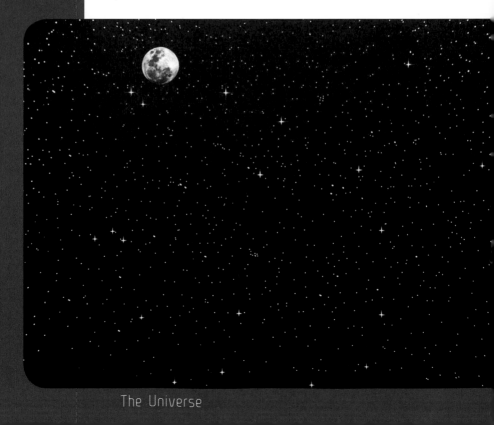

This image of the Moon's surface was taken by the Galileo *spacecraft. The image shows the dark areas on the Moon's surface, which are filled with lava.*

(115°C) during the day to a frigid –260°F (–160°C) at night. The Moon is 2,160 miles (3,475 km) in diameter—about one-quarter the size of Earth.

The Moon is Earth's closest neighbor. As the Moon orbits our planet, its gravity pulls on Earth, causing the ocean waters to rise and fall every day. This produces high tides (where the water rises highest and farthest onto the shores) and low tides (where the water level reaches its lowest point and part of the shore is dry).

Did You Know?

When you look up at the Moon, you may see the famous "man in the Moon"—the features of a human face. But what you are actually seeing is a combination of light-colored highlands and large, lowland areas filled with dark lava.

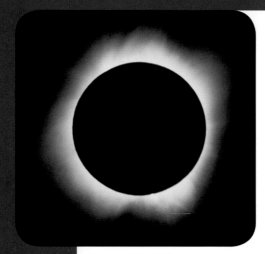

A total solar eclipse, shown here, occurs when the Moon passes between the Sun and Earth. The Moon blocks the light from the Sun, casting a shadow on Earth's surface.

Blackout

Imagine you're outside on a bright sunny day and the sunlight starts to disappear, getting dimmer and dimmer, until everything gets dark. Where did the Sun go? It's not hiding behind the clouds—there are no clouds. After a few minutes, the sunlight gradually returns, and it's a bright, beautiful day once again. What happened? It may have seemed like the end of the world for a moment, but it was actually a solar eclipse. The Moon, orbiting Earth, passed between the Sun and Earth and blocked the light, casting a dark shadow on Earth's surface.

During a solar eclipse, a bright halo can be seen around the darkened Sun. This is the Sun's outer atmosphere, called the corona. Never look directly

Mars: This planet is known as the "red planet" because the soil on Mars contains a lot of reddish-colored iron oxide (rust). Through telescopes, we can see this reddish surface from Earth. Dust in the planet's thin atmosphere makes the sky on Mars look pink.

Mars and Earth actually have a lot in common. Their days are nearly the same length, and like Earth, Mars has mountains, canyons, volcanoes, deserts, and polar caps. But no liquid water currently exists on the cold surface of Mars, where

at a solar eclipse. It can damage your eyes, even if you wear sunglasses. Special devices can be used to view solar eclipses safely. Eclipses can be total, when the Moon blocks the Sun completely; or partial, when only part of the Sun is blocked. A solar eclipse usually lasts for only a few minutes, although it can be as long as seven minutes.

The same kind of thing can happen to the Moon in the night sky. A lunar eclipse occurs when Earth is directly between the Sun and the Moon. A dark disk seems to move over the Moon, gradually covering it. What is actually happening is that the Moon is moving into Earth's shadow. During a lunar eclipse, the Moon does not usually become completely dark. It actually looks a little reddish.

temperatures do not rise above –24°F (–31°C). The only water is frozen in the polar ice caps at the north and south poles. Dry riverbeds on the surface of the planet indicate that Mars probably had running water millions of years ago. Discoveries in 2004 to 2008 suggest that there may be underground water on Mars as well.

These gullies on the surface of Mars indicate that the planet once had running water.

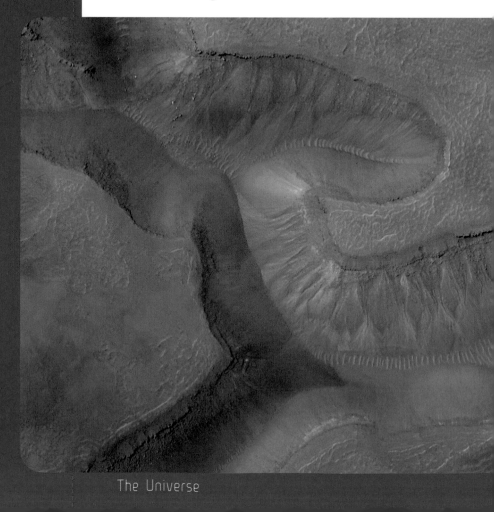

Mars's two moons, Deimos and Phobos, are not round like Earth's Moon. When our Moon formed millions of years ago, its gravity pulled in its material to make it round. But large moons have more gravity than smaller moons—and Deimos and Phobos are very small moons. They did not have enough gravity to round off their

This image of Phobos, one of Mars's moons, shows a giant crater on the lower right.

rough edges. They look like potatoes with craters.

Jupiter: Jupiter is the largest planet in the solar system. More than one thousand Earths could fit inside a globe the size of Jupiter! This giant planet also has a mass that is two and a half times greater than all the other planets combined. Unlike the inner planets, Jupiter has no solid surface. Instead, it is made mainly of gas and liquid, with a small rocky core.

Jupiter gives off more heat than it receives from the Sun. Apparently, this planet used to be larger, and it continues to shrink. As it contracts, it releases large amounts of energy. The temperature in Jupiter's inner core may be as much as 43,000°F (24,000°C).

The heat radiating from Jupiter's core (rather than the Sun) powers the planet's weather. The swirling clouds that surround Jupiter form colorful bands that are made of high and low pressure systems. When these highs and lows meet,

Jupiter's Great Red Spot, which is three times the size of Earth's diameter, is made of red clouds that swirl around in an oval shape.

they produce large thunderstorms all over the planet. Its largest storm, known as the Great Red Spot, is like a hurricane with violent winds and a calm center. It was first spotted more than three hundred years ago, and it *still* rages on.

In 2006 astronomers noticed a second red spot on Jupiter. This raging storm was about half the size of the Great Red Spot and given the nickname Red Spot Junior. Actually, Red Spot Junior was originally a big *white* storm. It formed in 2000 after three small white spots collided to form one big storm. The storm didn't turn red until 2006. Then, in 2008, astronomers observed a *third* red spot on Jupiter. It was about half the size of Red Spot Junior. And it, too, started out as a white storm before it turned red.

Four of Jupiter's moons are about the size of Earth's Moon. They are called the Galilean moons because they were first discovered by Galileo. The other moons, many of which have only recently been discovered, are much too small to be seen with a simple telescope like the one Galileo used. Astronomers believe that some of these tiny moons were once asteroids that got too close to Jupiter and were caught by Jupiter's powerful gravity.

Saturn: Saturn is the second-largest planet in the solar system. The rings that wrap around its equator give this planet a unique appearance. Saturn's rings consist mostly of ice, along with rock and dust, which orbit around the planet. Sunlight is reflected from these icy materials, making the rings shine brightly. Saturn has seven large rings and thousands

Did You Know?

Four planets in the solar system have rings: Jupiter, Saturn, Uranus, and Neptune. But Saturn's rings are the only ones bright enough to be seen through a small telescope.

This close-up view of one of Saturn's rings was put together by NASA from separate images taken by the Voyager 2 *spacecraft.*

of thin ringlets. In addition, this gas giant has around sixty moons, and astronomers continue to discover new ones.

Like Jupiter, Saturn is a giant ball of gas, surrounded by clouds. It has no hard surface, except for a rocky inner core. And Saturn, too, generates energy from inside its core. Despite their huge size, both Jupiter and Saturn spin around on their axes very quickly, with a day less than half as long as Earth's.

Uranus: Uranus was the first planet to be discovered with a telescope. An amateur astronomer named William Herschel spotted the planet back in 1781, using a telescope he built himself. Uranus is a gas planet, covered by blue green clouds. The blue green color is caused by methane gas in its atmosphere.

Uranus spins differently from any other planet. Instead of spinning like a top as the others do, Uranus appears to be rolling on its side, like a marble. Some scientists believe that something may have hit Uranus billions of years ago that made it tip over. That collision may have knocked off material that formed some of the planet's moons and rings.

Neptune: Neptune is the windiest planet in the solar system. Like Jupiter and Saturn, Neptune produces tremendous amounts of energy in its inner

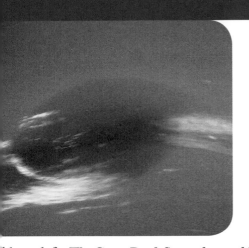

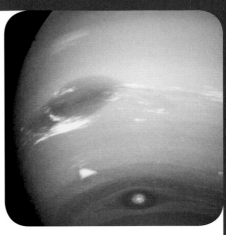

Above left: The Great Dark Spot, observed in 1989, was probably a deep hole in Neptune's clouds. It had disappeared in 1994 photos of the planet, but a new dark spot was seen in Neptune's northern hemisphere. **Above right:** *1989 photos also showed a fast-moving bright white cloud, nicknamed Scooter.*

core. As the heat moves through the atmosphere, it is swept along with Neptune's fast spinning. This produces strong winds, with speeds up to 1,200 miles (2,000 km) per hour, and stirs up tremendous storms.

Neptune is the last of the gas giants. It is also the coldest because of its great distance from the Sun. Triton, the largest of Neptune's thirteen moons, is covered with ice, with temperatures down to –391°F (–235°C).

Did You Know?

Photos taken by the spacecraft *Voyager 2* in 1989 showed a big dark spot the size of Earth and a small bright spot (Scooter). Both were moving eastward around the planet. But in 1994, photos taken with the Hubble telescope showed that both the Great Dark Spot and Scooter had vanished, and a new Great Dark Spot had appeared.

Asteroids, Meteors, and Comets

By the late 1700s, astronomers had calculated the orbits of all the known planets (from Mercury to Saturn). When they compared the distances of the planets from the Sun, the numbers seemed to form a regular pattern. When Uranus was discovered in 1781, it too fit into the pattern. But there was one problem: according to the formula, there should have been another planet between Mars and Jupiter.

For years, astronomers searched vainly for the "missing planet." What they found, instead, were countless rocks—some big and others very tiny. They called these rocks asteroids, from a Greek word for "starlike," because even through a powerful telescope, they look like tiny points of light.

Even though asteroids are not planets, they travel along their own orbits around the Sun. And like the planets, they rotate as they move. Most of the asteroids are found in a doughnut-shaped area, called the asteroid belt, which separates the inner and outer planets.

There are three types of asteroids: some are made of rock, some of metal, and some of both rock and metal. Asteroids come in all shapes and sizes, and they are usually irregular (not smooth and round). Even though there are millions of asteroids in outer space, most of them are very small, measuring only a few miles in diameter. But the largest asteroid, discovered in 2001, is as much as 788 miles (1,270 km) wide!

Where Did the Asteroids Come From?

Some astronomers believe that asteroids are leftovers that remained after the planets formed billions of years ago. Back then the asteroid belt may have included more than six hundred large asteroids that were unable to form one large planet. It's possible that Jupiter's strong gravity pulled on these big rocks, causing them to collide with one another. These rocks broke up into the millions of asteroids found in the asteroid belt today.

This illustration from NASA shows an asteroid belt around a star that is the same size and age as our Sun.

The orbits of some asteroids bring them close to Earth's orbit. In fact, a number of asteroids have actually hit Earth. Many scientists believe that an asteroid, about 6 to 12 miles (10 to 20 km) wide, crashed into Earth millions of years ago and eventually led to the extinction of the dinosaurs. When the asteroid hit, dust clouds filled the sky and became so thick that the Sun's light was blocked all over the planet. Earth got dark and cold. The plants soon died and so did the plant-eating animals. Eventually, the meat eaters also died because their food source disappeared. And the dinosaurs were gone forever.

This computer illustration shows fragments of a large asteroid colliding with Earth, which may have led to dinosaur extinction.

In 1980 scientists found evidence to support this asteroid theory. They discovered a huge crater, named Chicxulub, in Mexico. Rocks in the Chicxulub crater show evidence of a huge impact 65 million years ago, around the time that the dinosaurs became extinct.

Most of our "visitors" from the asteroid belt, however, are not whole asteroids. Instead, they are fragments (broken pieces) of asteroids that collided with one another. Such collisions are fairly frequent, and the impact may knock pieces of rock out of their orbit. The pull of gravity may send them hurtling in toward the inner planets. Mars has many craters formed by the impacts of asteroid fragments. So does Earth's Moon. But few fragments survive long enough to actually form craters on the surface of Earth. Our planet's atmosphere acts as a protective shield. Friction with air particles heats up the fast-moving chunks of rock to temperatures so high that they glow and are vaporized.

Every year, as much as 400,000 tons (363,000 metric tons) of cosmic material heads toward Earth. Fortunately, most of it burns up in Earth's atmosphere. Scientists call objects meteoroids before they reach Earth's atmosphere. If they burn up in the atmosphere, leaving a bright streak of light in the sky, they are known as meteors. Objects that pass through the atmosphere without burning up and reach Earth's surface are called meteorites.

Did You Know?

A meteor is also called a shooting star because it looks like a star falling from the sky.

Left: *A meteor streaks across the sky as the sun sets. If cosmic material makes it through Earth's atmosphere to Earth's surface, it is called a meteorite.* **Below:** *This crater was caused by a meterorite striking Earth in Arizona. The crater is 500 feet (152 meters) deep and 1 mile (1.6 km) across. It was created approximately fifty thousand years ago.*

When a meteorite hits the surface of a planet or moon, its impact produces a crater in it. More than one hundred meteor craters have been found on Earth's surface. Through the study of meteorites, scientists have gained information about the composition of the asteroids. Some of them are rich in iron, nickel, and other minerals.

How likely is it that we could have a *major* meteor impact? Objects like the one that may have caused the extinction of the dinosaurs strike Earth about once every 70 million years. Smaller objects come more often and can still cause a lot of damage. In 1908 a stony asteroid, about 130 feet (40 m) wide, exploded about 4 miles (6 km) above the surface of Siberia. Although it never even hit Earth, it produced a shock wave that knocked down trees over a 400-square-mile (1,036 sq. km) area.

Several teams of astronomers are tracking the movements of asteroids that travel near Earth. They hope to get an early warning of any incoming objects large enough to cause significant damage. If they can predict the probable sites of impact, emergency measures can be taken to save the lives of people in the area.

Some of the cosmic material that showers down on Earth comes from comets rather than asteroids. Comets usually orbit the Sun on the outskirts of the solar system. However, their orbits are so irregular that they sometimes come close to Earth.

Comets are a spectacular sight as their bright, glowing tails stretch out across the night sky. But they are quite different from meteors. A comet is like a dirty snowball made of snow, ice, and dust. Many scientists believe that comets are the leftovers of the icy gas planets Uranus and Neptune after they formed.

Halley's comet was named after an eighteenth-century British astronomer, Edmond Halley. While studying the reports of twenty-four comets that had been seen since 1337 and working out their orbits, Halley noticed that three of the comets, reported in 1531, 1607, and 1683, all had the same orbit. He believed that these three comets were actually the same one, which returned on a regular basis, and he predicted that its next visit would be in December 1758. Halley was right. The comet did return that year. Halley died in 1742 and was not alive to see it. Halley's comet last passed by Earth in 1986. Its next visit is due in 2061.

Some comets are believed to come from the Kuiper belt, a region beyond Neptune that contains at least seventy thousand icy, slow-moving objects in orbit around the Sun. (These objects range from 6 to 30 miles [10 to 50 km] in diameter.)

When a comet comes close to the Sun, the Sun's heat turns some of the snow and ice into a hot gas, which is blown by the solar wind to form a long, glowing tail pointed away from the Sun. Sometimes two or more tails appear. As the comet moves away from the Sun toward the cold outer edges of the solar system, its tail gradually disappears. Some comets are bright enough to be seen with the naked eye, while others cannot be seen without binoculars or a telescope.

> **Did You Know?**
>
> When it was closest to the Sun, the Great Comet of 1843 had a tail 300 million miles (475 million km) long, extending beyond the orbit of Mars.

chapter four

Starry Skies

When you look up at the sky on a clear night, you can see a spectacular display of stars. Some stars shine brightly, and others appear dim. But stars are so far away that—even with the most powerful telescope—they look like twinkling points of light.

The stars are not evenly spread out over the night sky like polka dots. There may be large numbers of them in some parts of the sky and very few in others. Out in space, stars are grouped together in large clusters, the galaxies. All the stars we see at night are in our galaxy, the Milky Way. This galaxy is made up of billions of stars.

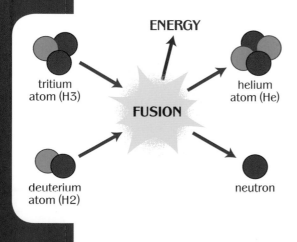

This diagram shows one of the nuclear fusion reactions that fuel the stars. The common form of hydrogen atom has a single proton in its nucleus. Here, two rarer forms, deuterium (1 proton + 1 neutron) and tritium (1 proton + 2 neutrons) fuse (join) to form a helium atom. Energy and a neutron are released in the reaction.

All the stars we see in the night sky are in the Milky Way galaxy. The brightest light in this night sky is the planet Venus. For more about why Venus is so bright in our sky, see page 60 in this chapter.

What Is a Star?

A star is a huge ball of glowing gas, made mostly of hydrogen and helium. Inside the star's core, nuclear fusion takes place: Hydrogen atoms crash into one another and combine (fuse) to form larger atoms of helium. The reaction also generates a lot of energy, which is released in the form of heat and light. Fusion reactions actually change matter into energy. So as energy is generated, matter is destroyed.

Did You Know?

Most stars have companions—they occur in pairs, triplets, or clusters. The Sun, however, exists on its own.

Astronomers classify stars into five groups, according to their size: (1) supergiants, (2) giants, (3) medium-size stars, (4) white dwarfs, and (5) neutron stars. Supergiants are the largest stars. They can be as much as one thousand times the diameter of the Sun. (Remember that the Sun's diameter is 865,000 miles [1.4 million km].) Giants have diameters that may range from ten to one hundred times that of the Sun. Medium-size stars are also known as main-sequence stars. They are about the same size as the Sun.

White dwarfs are small stars. White dwarfs may be as small as 5,200 miles (8,370 km) in diameter. Neutron stars are the tiniest stars. They actually have the same mass as the Sun, but they are very compact and measure just 10 miles (16 km) in diameter.

Starlight

Much of what scientists know about stars came from studying our own star, the Sun. Like the Sun, all stars give off light energy. Light can provide a lot of information. By analyzing the light given off by a star, scientists can figure out its brightness, temperature, and color. Closer examinations can show what a star is made of, how much it weighs, how fast it is going, and its position in the sky.

How do scientists learn about stars just by studying their light? The sunlight you see shining brightly outside is known as white light, or visible light. Back in 1666, Sir Isaac Newton discovered that white light actually contains all the colors of the rainbow. In an experiment, Newton allowed a beam of sunlight to hit an angled piece of glass called a prism. The light broke up into a rainbow of colors that blended into one another. Newton called this band of colors a spectrum. When the sun comes out after a storm, the raindrops still floating in the air act like prisms. As the sunlight hits the raindrops, these little "prisms" split the Sun's rays into a spectrum. The rainbow contains bands of colors: red, orange, yellow, green, blue, and violet.

As sunlight showers over Earth, it moves in waves at incredibly fast speeds. These light waves are also called electromagnetic waves because they are made up of electrical and magnetic fields that travel together. The electrical field moves up and down, while the magnetic field moves back and forth. Visible light is just one form of electromagnetic radiation and belongs to a much larger spectrum of energy called the electromagnetic spectrum.

All the colors in the electromagnetic spectrum can be seen in this rainbow after a rainstorm.

Stars can give off a wide range of electro-magnetic radiation. The type of radiation a star gives off depends on its temperature: the hotter the star, the more energy it gives off. The hottest stars look blue, and the coolest ones are red. Others have colors in between. In fact, astronomers have classified stars into a whole spectrum of color types using the letters O, B, A, F, G, K, and M, where O is the hottest and M is the coolest. Each type, in turn, has ten subdivisions numbered from 0 to 9, with 9 being the coolest.

What Is a Light-Year?

You probably figure out distances to or from your home all the time. Your school is about 2 miles (3.2 km) away, the nearest shopping mall is roughly 6 miles (10 km) away, or your aunt lives 180 miles (290 km) away. But the universe is so enormous that measuring distances in miles or kilometers would not be very useful. The numbers would be too large and very complicated. For example, Andromeda, the closest galaxy, is nearly 10 quintillion miles (16 quintillion km) away. Imagine having to write it out: that's 10,000,000,000,000,000,000 miles. Instead, astronomers use units called light-years to measure the distance of stars and other objects in outer space.

Electromagnetic Spectrum

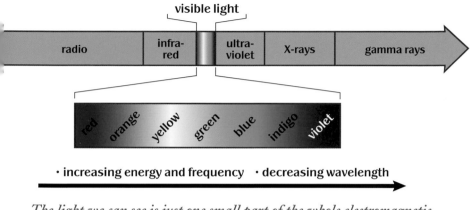

The light we can see is just one small part of the whole electromagnetic spectrum.

A light-year is the distance that light travels in one year. Light always travels 186,000 miles (300,000 km) per second, so in one year, light can travel 5.88 trillion miles (9.46 trillion km). Andromeda is thus about 2 million light-years from Earth.

We never get to see stars the way they are right now. They are too far away, and light takes time to travel these huge distances. So if a star is ten light-years away, we are actually seeing what the star looked like ten years ago. If it suddenly exploded at any moment, we would not find out about it for another ten years.

Our Sun, a yellow star, is classified as G2. So while we think of the Sun as unimaginably hot, it's not even among the hotter half of the spectral types. The hottest stars—the O types, which are up to 72,000°F (40,000°C)—are more than seven times as hot as our Sun.

Astronomers also use another scale to classify stars: magnitude, which is based on brightness. The magnitude scale goes from –4 to +22. The lowest numbers are the brightest, and the highest numbers

Stargazing

How can we learn about things that are light-years away? Optical telescopes work by gathering light from objects and turning it into an image. They use glass lenses or mirrors to bend light rays so that the object seems much larger. An instrument called a spectroscope can be used to analyze starlight seen through a telescope. The spectroscope breaks down light into a pattern of lines (a spectrum) showing the types of electromagnetic radiation it gives off.

The light from a star contains information not only about what it's made of but also about its motion. Bands in a star's spectrum change depending on

are the faintest. Sirius, the Dog Star, is the brightest star in the sky, and has a magnitude of –1 (the brightest object in the sky apart from the Sun is the planet Venus, with a magnitude of –4). The faintest stars that can be seen with the naked eye are a magnitude of +6. With binoculars we can see to about +9. The faintest stars that have been photographed through powerful telescopes have a magnitude of +22. Our closest neighbor in the Milky Way, Alpha Centauri, has a magnitude of –0.3. It is actually a triple star: a G2, a K1, and an M5 that are clustered close together about 4.4 light-years from us.

whether it is moving toward or away from Earth. Light radiation from an object moving away shifts toward the red end of the spectrum (a red shift). The light from an object moving toward us shows a blue shift. The amount of the shift indicates the speed of the movement. This shifting of the spectrum is called the Doppler effect.

The radio telescope takes advantage of another type of radiation given off by stars: radio waves. With computers, scientists can turn a star's radio signals into a picture that we can see. Radio telescopes can produce images of much more distant stars than those that can be seen with an Earth-based optical telescope.

The brightness of an object in the sky depends on a number of different things. One is its energy: the hotter the star, the brighter it is. And yet, Venus is the brightest object in our night sky (except for the Moon), but it is nowhere near as hot as a star. So distance is also important in determining how bright an object appears to us. Closer objects may seem brighter than distant ones even if their temperature is lower. Dust clouds can also block the light of stars, making them appear dimmer.

A Star Is Born

Stars do not give off light forever. Although a star is not a living thing, it does have a life cycle that includes birth, life, and death. The energy generated in a star's core keeps it shining brightly until its hydrogen and helium are used up, and eventually it burns out. Most stars are billions of years old, but new ones are forming all the time. Our skies are filled with young stars, middle-aged stars, and old stars.

A star starts out inside a nebula—a cloud of dust and gas (mostly hydrogen). Large amounts of dust and gas are pulled together by gravity, creating a thick cloud. Hydrogen atoms start smashing into one another, and they get extremely hot. The cloud starts to shrink into a ball, which continues to get hotter. Eventually, the center becomes so hot that temperatures reach millions of degrees—hot enough for fusion reactions to take place. Soon the hot gases forming the star's core can generate enough energy to radiate large amounts of light. And a star is born.

Extrasolar Planets

After our star, the Sun, was born, a number of planets formed and began to move in orbits around it. Astronomers have wondered whether this was an unusual event or a common process. Extrasolar planets (ones orbiting other stars) cannot be seen even with the most powerful telescopes. But their gravitational pull causes a wobble in the motion of the stars they orbit—and that is something astronomers *can* detect. The first extrasolar planet was discovered in 1995, orbiting a G-type star in the constellation Pegasus. By mid-2008, about three hundred other planets had been found in other star systems. Most of these planets are gas giants close to Saturn's size or larger. Astronomers believe there are many smaller, more Earth-like planets too.

New stars are made in the Eagle Nebula. The nebula is about seven thousand light-years from Earth. The brightest star in the nebula can be seen from Earth with binoculars.

A star has to keep burning its hydrogen supply to continue to shine brightly. It can take millions or billions of years for a star to use up all its fuel. But as it gets older and the hydrogen supply dwindles, the star goes through some changes. Even though the star is gradually losing energy, it doesn't just fizzle out and disappear. Instead, it blows up like a balloon and turns into a huge, red ball called a red giant. Its diameter may grow to a hundred times its original size, but its outer temperature is much lower. Its inner core is even hotter than before, however.

Temperatures and pressures are so high inside a red giant's core that it can start

using a new fuel for fusion reactions: helium, found deep
inside the core. This would keep a medium-size star going
for another 100 million years or more. As the star cools, its
outer layers slowly spread out into a glowing gas shell, and the
core becomes smaller and smaller.

Gradually, the shell fades away,
and the star shrinks down to a
white dwarf—the hot remains
of the star's core. Over billions
of years, a white dwarf will
eventually cool and disappear
until it becomes a black dwarf,
which no longer gives off light.

Did You Know?

A brown dwarf is a
"failed star." It looks
like a tiny faint star,
but it never becomes
a true star.

Stars that have a mass more
than eight times that of the
Sun have a more dramatic death. These massive stars turn
into supergiants. They are hotter than red giants. In fact,
supergiants can get so hot that carbon and oxygen (products
of helium fusion) can react further. These nuclear reactions
form atoms of heavy elements, such as iron. The iron builds
up in the core. Eventually, the core becomes so heavy that
it collapses. This sets off some reactions that produce even
heavier elements until there is a massive explosion, and the star
becomes a supernova.

If the remains of the star are less than three times
the mass of the Sun, it becomes compressed and forms
a neutron star. This rapidly spinning star is also called a
pulsar, because it sends out pulses of radio waves at regular
intervals. These radio signals can be picked up by large
radio receivers on Earth.

If the remains of an exploding star are more than three times the mass of the Sun, the star's core collapses and forms a black hole. Black holes are one of the most intriguing mysteries of the universe. A black hole is a dark region in space that exerts a tremendous force of gravity. It is like a gigantic vacuum cleaner, sucking in anything that gets too close—a star, a planet, or a cloud of gas. Any matter that enters a black hole is crushed and stretched out by the powerful gravity until it disappears into nothingness. Not even light can escape a black hole, so it remains dark and invisible.

Although astronomers cannot see black holes, they can locate them by watching the effect they have on nearby objects. For instance, gas from a star may be pulled onto a disk that spins around the black hole. The swirling gases start to heat up and send out X-rays that can be picked up by artificial satellites in orbit around Earth. Astronomers first observed evidence of a black hole back in 1971 using the world's first X-ray satellite. They named this black hole Cygnus X-1. Earth is in no danger of being sucked down this black hole—it's about eight thousand light-years away.

Supernova remnants, the remains of explosions, have some important effects. As the shock wave from the explosion moves outward, it heats and stirs up any matter it meets in the spaces between stars. The moving shock wave sends heavy metals through the galaxy, providing raw materials for the formation of new stars. It also speeds up the movements of charged particles to nearly the speed of light. Astronomers believe that this is the source of cosmic rays.

Dark Matter and Other Mysteries

Back in 1933, an astronomer named Fritz Zwicky estimated the total mass of some distant galaxies according to measurements of their brightness. But then, using a different method to calculate the mass of the same group of galaxies, he got a result that was four hundred times as large. These puzzling findings became known as the "missing mass problem" and remained a scientific curiosity for several decades.

Swiss astronomer Fritz Zwicky came across the missing mass problem in science. Here, in 1956, he shows on a blackboard how the planet Jupiter could be thrown out of orbit.

By the 1970s, however, scientists were beginning to realize that some of their own observations could be explained only by assuming that the universe contains large amounts of matter that we cannot see. In fact, astronomers can see only about 10 percent of the amount of mass that would account

for the movements of stars in a galaxy. They can get clues about this dark matter from the X-rays released by the clouds of hot gases in which the galaxies float, but they are not yet sure just what it is. Dark matter may be made up of very faint stars, black holes, gas, and dust. These are ordinary things that simply do not send out enough radiation for today's instruments to detect. Or dark matter could contain unusual particles that have never been observed. Whatever

The dark matter in this NASA image is highlighted artificially in magenta. This image was taken by a powerful telescope in South America. NASA scientists were able to map the dark matter by using observations of the same area by the Hubble Space Telescope.

What Is a Quasar?

A quasar is the most distant object in the universe that astronomers can observe with a high-powered telescope. It gives off huge amounts of light energy, as well as radio waves, X-rays, and infrared radiation. Quasars are very bright out in space. From Earth they look like faint stars because they are so far away. (The brightest quasar that can be seen from Earth is 1.8 billion light-years away.) A quasar is not a single star. Astronomers believe it is the glowing center of a faraway galaxy.

it is, dark matter provides some of the gravity that gives the galaxies their shape and holds them together. But dark matter alone can account for only about one-third of these effects. Astronomers believe that something else—"dark energy"—is helping to shape the universe. According to astronomer David N. Spergel, of Princeton University in New Jersey, the universe consists of about 23 percent dark matter, 4 percent ordinary matter, and 73 percent dark energy.

Dark energy also seems to be speeding up the motions of the stars and galaxies. Such movements have already caused a number of collisions between galaxies. When two galaxies collide, they may join to form a new, larger galaxy. (Astronomers believe that our Milky Way formed in this manner.) If one of the colliding galaxies is much larger than the other, however, its gravity may pull the smaller galaxy apart, using its remains as raw materials to form huge numbers of new stars.

The Andromeda galaxy is our closest galaxy neighbor in the universe—and it is two million light-years away!

Observations of star movements suggest that our Milky Way is heading for another collision, with our neighbor Andromeda. These two galaxies are expected to merge to form a giant elliptical galaxy. But that won't happen for another five billion years.

Less than five billion years after that, the Milky Way will take over two other neighboring galaxies, the Magellanic Clouds.

Meanwhile, though, the universe also seems to be expanding at a faster rate. Stars and galaxies are moving apart faster than when the open universe theory was first introduced. If these observations are correct, distant galaxies will eventually move out too far to be observed. By 150 billion years from now, the sky will be mostly dark and empty. After 100 trillion years, all the gas and dust in interstellar space will be used up, and no new stars will be formed.

The Magellanic Clouds are a pair of galaxies near the Milky Way.

Constellations

The ancient Greeks looked up at the sky filled with stars and linked various groups of them together to form the outlines of people, animals, and objects. The patterns they formed are called constellations, from the Latin words meaning "together" and "stars." Some of the constellations we recognize were named thousands of years ago. If you look up at the night sky, you, too, can see what ancient astronomers saw by playing your own connect-the-dots game. Of course, there's no real link between the actual stars. Constellations are formed from our imagination.

Astronomers have named eighty-eight constellations. Each has its own designated spot in the sky, where it can be found night after night. The constellations appear to move across the sky as the night goes by, but that's only because Earth is turning on its axis. Their positions also change over the course of the year, but the arrangement of constellations on the sky map stays the same. So different constellations will be directly overhead at different times of the year.

Did You Know?

The stars in a constellation look as though they are close to one another. Actually, they're not. Some of the stars are much farther from Earth than others. For instance, the star at the tip of the Big Dipper's handle is 198 light-years from Earth, and the one next to it is just 78 light-years away.

Astronomers have made star maps to locate various stars and to find their way around the sky. Sailors have used star maps to help them navigate the ocean waters. The North Star, Polaris, is often used as a reference point for north. It is the brightest star in the Little Dipper and belongs to the constellation Ursa Minor (Latin for "little bear").

The Big Dipper constellation can be seen in the top of this image. Northern lights can also be seen in the sky.

Different constellations can be seen in different parts of the world. Some constellations can be seen only in the Northern Hemisphere and others only in the Southern Hemisphere. Some can be seen in both hemispheres.

As Earth moves along its orbit, the position of the Sun seems to change against the background of the stars. The path of the Sun's apparent movement is called the ecliptic. (Of course, the Sun is not really moving. We are just looking at it from different angles as we move around it over the course of a year.) A band of twelve constellations that lie on the ecliptic make up the zodiac, a Greek word for "circle of animals." The zodiac constellations lie at the boundary between the northern and southern skies; they can be seen in both hemispheres. The zodiac is also known as the birth-sign constellations.

chapter five

Exploring the Universe

"That's one small step for man, one great leap for mankind." These were the words of U.S. astronaut Neil Armstrong on July 20, 1969, as he stepped onto the surface of the Moon. This was the first human landing on any planet or satellite outside planet Earth. To the millions who watched on television, it was like science fiction come to life.

Since ancient times, people have dreamed about leaving planet Earth and exploring other worlds. We have come a long way since 1609, when Galileo first used a simple telescope to study the sky. We have sophisticated methods that allow scientists to collect information and learn more about our universe. Powerful telescopes provide clear pictures of distant planets and stars. Artificial satellites orbit Earth and send back various kinds of information to let us know what's going on around the planet. Spacecraft can travel to outer space. Some carry human pilots and passengers—astronauts. Others carry telescopes, cameras, and other instruments that send back pictures and other information. Self-directed robots are exploring other planets of the solar system.

The Space Race

The space age really got started on October 4, 1957, when the Soviet Union (a union of fifteen republics that included Russia) launched *Sputnik*, the first artificial satellite to orbit Earth. The satellite launching was made possible by years of intensive work on rocket development. This work began in Germany in the 1930s. During World War II (1939–1945), Nazi Germany launched

This was the first official picture of the Soviet satellite Sputnik 1 *released in 1957.*

V-2 rockets filled with explosives against Great Britain and Belgium. Engineer Wernher von Braun was a leader in the German rocket program. After the war, he moved to the United States. Later, he headed the U.S. rocket program at NASA.

After World War II, both the United States and the Soviet Union worked to develop rockets that could travel from one continent to the other. These rockets were intended as weapons that could reach their target without refueling. While traveling such long distances, the rockets reached heights of more than 50 miles (80 km) above Earth's surface. They actually entered the beginning of outer space. The Soviet team was the first to use a rocket to launch a satellite that traveled in an orbit around Earth.

Instead of explosives, the rocket satellite launcher carried a small aluminum sphere with radio transmitters.

The launching of *Sputnik 1* brought enormous publicity to the Soviet Union. Just a few months later, however, the United States successfully launched a more sophisticated satellite, *Explorer 1*, on January 31, 1958. The instruments it carried transmitted the first information about the Van Allen belt. Later, a U.S. satellite produced the first photo of Earth from orbit, and a satellite launched by the Soviet Union transmitted pictures of the Moon's farside, which had never before been seen by humans.

In 1961 the Soviets sent up the first human, cosmonaut Yuri Gagarin, to orbit Earth on a

Soviet cosmonaut Yuri Gagarin was the first human to be sent up in space. He orbited Earth in a spaceship in 1961.

spaceship. The following year, astronaut John Glenn Jr. became the first American to orbit Earth.

The space race between the Soviet Union and the United States continued. The next big goal was to land a man on the Moon. The United States won that race after a huge national effort that was launched in 1961. The historic Moon landing in 1969 was part of the Apollo project.

Above: In 1962 U.S. astronaut John Glenn Jr. was the first American to orbit Earth. He went up in space again in 1998. **Below:** *Apollo astronaut Neil Armstrong was the first human to set foot on the Moon.*

The spacecraft developed and used in this project included a command module, which remained in orbit around the Moon, and a lunar module, which actually landed. Rockets lifted the lunar module back into orbit, where it docked with the command module for the return trip to Earth. The United States made five more Moon landings, but the Soviet lunar program had a series of problems and was unable to launch a successful piloted Moon flight.

Meanwhile, the Soviets were successfully developing a space station, called Salyut. A space station is an orbiting structure containing living and working space. It's like a home in space where people can conduct studies on the physical and psychological conditions in space, such as weightlessness, extreme temperatures, and low air pressure. They can also observe Earth and the Sun from orbit, and they can look out into space, as well.

A series of Salyuts were launched into orbit. During this time, the United States launched its own space station, Skylab, in 1973. It remained in orbit until 1979. Mir, a

The space shuttle **Atlantis** *departs from the Mir Russian space station in 1995. The United States started joint missions to Mir that year.*

Soviet space station, was the first one designed to be made up of units, or modules, which could be joined together while in orbit. The first module was launched in 1986, and additional ones were added over the next ten years. Some cosmonauts lived and worked there for more than a year. Joint U.S.–Russian missions were started in 1995. Seven U.S. astronauts lived aboard Mir for various periods of time.

NASA never accomplished its goal of building a permanent orbital space station. But an International Space Station project began in 1993. Sixteen nations, including the United States, Russia, Canada, Japan, Brazil, and the eleven nations of the European Space Agency, are taking part in the work.

The first module of the International Space Station (ISS) was launched in 1998. Scheduled to be completed in 2010, it

This photograph of the International Space Station was taken in 2008 by the space shuttle **Discovery.**

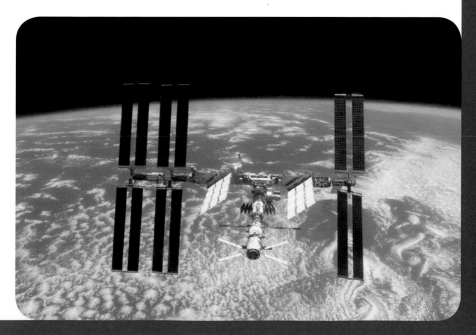

will be the largest space station ever—more than four times as large as Mir. It travels around Earth nearly sixteen times a day, at an average speed of 17,210 miles (27,700 km) per hour. Its orbit is about 217 miles (350 km) above the planet's surface. Crews of

Living in Space

Imagine living on a space station. Out in space, there is no feeling of gravity, no oxygen, no water, and no air pressure. And temperatures can go to extremes. It may take some getting used to, but astronauts are specially trained to handle living in such extreme conditions.

Space stations may not have all the comforts of home, but they are designed to support life for long periods of time. For example, life support systems generate oxygen for the astronauts to breathe. At the same time, the carbon dioxide they exhale is filtered out. The air pressure stays at levels close to the air pressure on Earth. The temperature is kept at a comfortable level, as well.

Imagine trying to sleep in weightless conditions. You would be floating around the cabin as soon as you

astronauts and researchers have been living at the station since November 2000. In addition, astronauts from sixteen countries and a number of civilian space tourists have visited the ISS. (As of 2008, a space station vacation for one person costs about twenty million dollars.)

relaxed. Astronauts avoid this by strapping themselves into their sleeping areas. They also have to wear eyeshades while they sleep because the Sun rises and sets every hour and a half as the spacecraft travels in its orbit around Earth.

Eating is also somewhat different than back on Earth. If an astronaut eats a ham sandwich, for example, bits of food might fly away. So some of the food is freeze-dried, with water added just before eating. Other meals are packaged in sealed bags that are squeezed to release the contents.

Exercise is actually very important out in space. Weightless conditions for too long can lead to bone loss and weakened muscles. So astronauts do special exercises to keep their bodies strong and healthy.

The ISS has research laboratories for studying the effects of space conditions on people. The station also has materials and instruments for testing manufacturing methods that cannot be used on Earth. For example, flames burn differently and materials mix differently in the absence of gravity. Space factories may someday make better materials for computer chips and other high-tech applications. Researchers are also studying the nature of space and very low-gravity conditions. Such studies may bring new insights into the nature of gravity itself and how the universe developed.

A key to the success of the space station was the development of the space shuttle, a reusable spacecraft that could carry people up to space stations and bring them back. The space shuttle can be used over and over, making it much more cost-effective than "throwaway" rockets. When U.S. engineers started this project in the early 1970s, they wanted to design a machine that would be able to take off like a rocket and land like an airplane. In 1981 they successfully launched and landed the first space shuttle, *Columbia*.

Space shuttle missions have become an important part of the space program. The shuttles are used to carry people back and forth from space stations, and they can put artificial satellites and space probes into orbit around Earth. They also retrieve artificial satellites that need to be serviced.

NASA plans to retire the three remaining space shuttles in 2010. In the final launch, in May 2010,

Above: *Astronaut Greg Chamitoff floats in the International Space Station in 2008. Chamitoff and other astronauts arrived at the station aboard space shuttle* Discovery. Discovery *lifted off on its space mission in May 2008* (right).

the space shuttle *Endeavor* will deliver spare parts to the International Space Station. After that, NASA plans to purchase seats on the Russian *Soyuz* spacecrafts until 2015. They expect the new Orion spacecraft to be ready to take over shuttle service and space exploration by then.

Exploring Other Worlds

Much of what we know about our solar system has been discovered by space probes. A space probe, which is launched by a rocket or a space shuttle, is an unpiloted machine designed to collect information about neighboring planets, moons, comets, and even asteroids. Space probes usually do not return to Earth. They may fly by a planet, go into orbit around it, or land on its surface. Probes are equipped with high-tech instruments, which survey the target and send information back to Earth. They have also provided close-up views of planets, moons, asteroids, and even a streaking comet.

The *Mariner 10* probe, launched in 1973, was the first spacecraft to visit Mercury. It sent back the first close-up photos of both Venus and Mercury. It also sent back data on the atmosphere, surface, and other characteristics of the two planets. The *MESSENGER* mission, launched in 2004, went into orbit around Mercury in January 2008. It sent back the first photos of the other side of the planet and also studied Mercury's chemical composition, geology, and magnetic field.

The wealth of information provided by space probes can also help in planning other space missions. Some space probes have to be specially designed to withstand the harsh environments of other planets. For example, a space probe that visits Venus must be tough enough to withstand the acid in the planet's clouds. Scientists also found out firsthand how powerful the air pressure on Venus is. When space probes first tried to land on Venus, the probes were crushed. Later, engineers created probes that could handle the crushing pressure of Venus at least long enough to send some pictures of Venus's surface back to Earth.

Many science-fiction films depict Earth being attacked by aliens from outer space. These aliens are usually little green men from Mars. But in real life, space probes visiting Mars have not found any signs of life. Some scientists believe that there may have been life on Mars at one time because of the dry riverbeds found on its surface. In 1997 the *Pathfinder* space probe landed on Mars, where it took pictures of the surface and collected samples of dust and rock. It also carried the *Sojourner* rover, a six-wheel remote-controlled car designed to explore Mars's rocky surface and take pictures.

A later probe landed two Mars Exploration rovers on the surface of the planet in January 2004. The two rovers, *Spirit*

*The **Spirit** rover took this image from the top of a hill on Mars during its mission in 2005. A part of the rover is visible on the bottom of the image.*

and *Opportunity*, were mobile robots that could climb hills and crawl down into craters. They found evidence that a salty sea once covered much of the planet's surface. Their mission was supposed to last only ninety days, but they were still going strong in June 2008, when a new probe, the *Phoenix*, landed at the planet's north pole. The *Phoenix*'s mission was to send back photos and test the Martian soil and ice. *Phoenix* found the mineral calcium carbonate in surface deposits. (This mineral is formed in the

The **Phoenix** *probe attempts to pick up soil* (bottom of photo) *on Mars for tests in June 2008.*

presence of water.) *Phoenix* also detected traces of snow in clouds high above Mars's northern plains.

Meanwhile, photos taken by NASA's Mars Global Surveyor revealed new deposits of minerals that appeared some time between 2001 and 2004. These deposits extend hundreds of yards long. Scientists believe they were left by liquid water that welled up from underground and flowed downhill before evaporating. These discoveries suggest that living organisms may actually exist underground on Mars.

Pioneer 10 and *11* were the first space probes to reach Jupiter. They sent back the first close-up pictures of Jupiter in the early 1970s. *Pioneer 10* also discovered that Jupiter had a tremendous magnetic field—about twenty thousand times stronger than Earth's! In 1979 *Voyager 1* sent back the first photos of Jupiter's ring system. The *Galileo* space probe, which arrived at Jupiter in 1995, made a direct study of Jupiter's atmosphere, conducted close-up examinations of the larger moons, and determined that Jupiter's rings were formed from dust particles thrown out into space by impacts of meteorites on its moons.

The Pluto Express

Pluto may not be considered a planet anymore, but that doesn't mean that scientists have forgotten about it. In 2006 NASA sent out *New Horizons*, a fast-moving probe bound for Pluto. The probe passed close by Jupiter in 2007 and sent back new data and photos of this giant planet. Scheduled to reach Pluto in 2015, *New Horizons* will take pictures of Pluto and its three moons.

Three space probes have flown past Saturn. *Voyager 2* took close-up photos of Saturn's rings in 1981 as it headed toward Uranus and Neptune. The probe showed that the rings are made up of thousands of rings close together. In 2004 the *Cassini* probe became the first spacecraft to study Saturn's system of rings and moons from the planet's orbit. In January 2005, the *Huygens* probe landed on the surface of Titan, Saturn's largest moon. The high-tech instruments on both spacecraft have provided scientists with important data and fascinating views.

One of the most successful space probes is the Hubble Space Telescope. Unlike telescopes on Earth, the Hubble Space Telescope works in outer space. It has a number of advantages over ground-based telescopes.

When you look through a ground-based telescope, the image may not appear as clear as you'd like. That's because light from the stars and planets must pass through Earth's atmosphere. Besides clouds and dust particles, the atmosphere contains water vapor and rippling wind currents. These all distort the light rays and make the image seen through a telescope fuzzy and unclear. The lights in cities also produce a glow in the night sky that makes it harder to see objects out in space. All these difficulties are avoided by placing a telescope on a satellite out in space where there is no atmosphere.

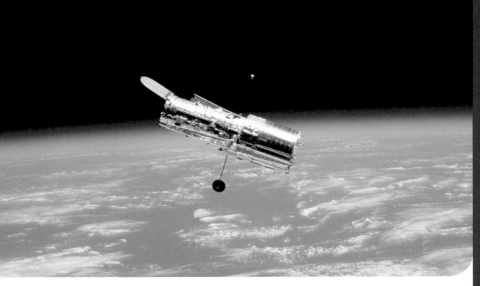

The Hubble Space Telescope orbits above Earth.

Since it was sent into orbit in 1990, Hubble has produced clearer pictures of planets, stars, and other objects than any telescope on Earth. It has even located distant galaxies that had never been seen by any telescope on Earth.

The Space Age

1945 German rocket engineer Wernher von Braun emigrates to the United States.

1957 The Soviet Union launches *Sputnik*, the first artificial satellite to orbit Earth.

1958 NASA is established.
The United States launches its first satellite, *Explorer 1*, which reveals the Van Allen belt.
U.S. satellite *Vanguard 1* shows that Earth is slightly flattened at the poles.

1959 U.S. satellite *Explorer 6* transmits the first photo of Earth from space.
Soviet satellite *Luna 2* lands on the Moon.
Soviet satellite *Luna 3* transmits photos of the farside of the Moon.

1961 Soviet cosmonaut Yuri Gagarin becomes the first human to orbit Earth.
The United States launches a project to put a man on the Moon.

1962 U.S. astronaut John Glenn Jr. becomes the first American to orbit Earth.

1969 U.S. astronaut Neil Armstrong becomes the first human to land on the Moon.

1971 The Soviet Union launches *Salyut 1*, the first orbital space station.

1972   *Pioneer 10* space probe passes through the asteroid belt and sends back photos of Jupiter.

1973   *Pioneer 11* space probe makes the first close-up observations of Saturn.

The United States launches its first space station, Skylab.

1979   *Voyager 1* space probe transmits first photos of Jupiter's rings.

1981   *Voyager 2* transmits close-ups of Saturn's rings and observations of Uranus and Neptune.

1986   The Soviet Union launches the first module of space station Mir.

1990   Hubble Space Telescope is sent up into orbit.

1993   Construction of a permanent orbital space station is made an international project.

1995   Joint U.S.-Soviet space missions started.

Galileo space probe sent to orbit Jupiter and sends close-ups of Jupiter's rings.

1997   *Pathfinder* probe carrying robot explorer lands on Mars.

1998   First module of International Space Station is launched.

2004   *Cassini* space probe reaches Saturn

2005   *Huygens* probe lands on Titan's surface.

2006   *New Horizons* probe observes Jupiter on its way to Pluto.

2008   *Phoenix* probe lands on Mars and finds evidence of water.

chapter six

Our Future in the Universe

Why is it so important that we study the universe? Some people think the whole space program is a waste of time and money. With so many unsolved problems on Earth, why should we pour billions of dollars into sending up satellites and spacecraft? What difference does it make whether there is water on Mars or how many moons Saturn has? And the stars are so far away! Even close to the speed of light, it would take longer than a human lifetime to travel to them.

First of all, the space effort has brought many benefits right here on Earth. In addition to creating jobs and boosting the economy, the space industry has produced inventions (spinoffs) that have improved things that we use every day. For example, Velcro fasteners were originally developed to keep things from floating around inside a spacecraft. Now we use Velcro to fasten shoes and clothing. The Teflon coating that keeps food from sticking to pots and pans was first used in space to help machine parts move smoothly.

Space Program Spinoffs

Have you ever wondered, *What good is the space program?* Take a look at all the wonderful inventions that we have in our lives thanks to the space program:

- TV satellite dish
- Computed tomography (CT), magnetic resonance imaging (MRI), and positron emission tomography (PET) scans—computer programs developed by NASA make images of the body clearer
- Vision screening computer systems
- Ear thermometers that detect heat energy
- Firefighter suits made of fire-resistant fabrics
- Smoke detectors
- Cordless tools, such as vacuum cleaners, drills, edge trimmers
- Shock-absorbing helmets
- Invisible braces for teeth
- Joystick controllers

Orbiting satellites are providing a wealth of information, not only about our near and distant neighbors but also about Earth. Weather satellites have greatly improved the accuracy of predicting the weather. Satellites have also revealed the locations of deposits of valuable minerals and other resources. Spy satellites provide valuable military information, such as troop movements and missile locations.

A weather satellite orbits around Earth. Many different kinds of satellites are used to provide information to researchers on Earth.

Exploring the universe is an enormous intellectual adventure as well, satisfying the curiosity that people have felt ever since they first looked up at the sky. It is also an investment in the future. For example, other planets in our solar system, moons, and even asteroids may be important sources for mining metals and other minerals in future centuries. Our descendants may someday explore the planets in our solar system and those of distant stars. They may build colonies on other Earth-like worlds or learn to adapt themselves to new environments. Perhaps we could survive on Mars, for instance, by building dome cities inside airtight, watertight enclosures containing all the necessities for life. Spacecraft could take us from one dome city to another.

Although our knowledge of the universe has been growing steadily, many mysteries still remain. One of the greatest mysteries is whether there is an intelligent life in outer space. Could we be alone in a universe that contains trillions of stars? We have already found other stars that have planets. The conditions that produced our planet and its life are similar to those in other star systems. Some experts believe it is possible that life could exist elsewhere too.

Listening for Life

Special agencies, such as the Search for Extraterrestrial Intelligence (SETI), have organized programs all over the world for people to search for life in outer space. Most of their efforts are involved in sending out radio signals to distant stars in hopes of getting some sign that we are not alone. Many scientists believe that radio signals are the best way to communicate across the great distances of space. So far, there is no evidence of life outside Earth. But the possibilities are mind-boggling. Members of SETI believe that finding another civilization will change our views of our place in the universe.

Goldilocks Planets

Astronomers believe that if there is life in other star systems, it will be found on Earth-like planets. They must have an orbit that is not too close or too far away from their sun. Planets that orbit very close to their sun (such as Mercury in our solar system) would be too hot to support life. Those in distant orbits are too cold. Like Goldilocks in the Three Bears' house, living organisms need an environment that is "just right." Planets at a distance similar to Earth's orbit around the Sun would be warm enough to have liquid water.

SETI scientists study information in the SETI control room.

They would get enough energy to fuel the activities of living things, but not enough to burn them.

Astronomers have been looking for rocky planets within the "Goldilocks zone" of their star. In 2007 they discovered an Earth-like planet orbiting a red dwarf star, Gliese 581. The planet is about 50 percent larger than Earth but has about five times as much mass. Its orbit is much closer to its sun. A year on the planet lasts just thirteen Earth days. But its temperature would be "just right" because its sun is much cooler than ours.

We would be just "one member of a universal community of intelligent species."

If anybody out there is answering our radio calls, how will we know it? Signals from an alien civilization in another part of the galaxy would be very faint by the time they reached us. Only the largest radio antenna on Earth, the dish at Arecibo, Puerto Rico, is sensitive enough to pick them up. But there is so much background noise, from TV and radar signals on Earth to the radio emissions from distant quasars, that the call we are waiting for could easily be missed.

It takes a huge amount of computing power to analyze the incoming radio signals and screen out the background noise. A single computer could not handle that tremendous job.

Left: *The radio telescope at Arecibo, Puerto Rico, is the largest in the world.* Below: *The giant dish at Arecibo has been featured in television shows such as* The X-Files, *and movies such as* Contact *and the James Bond movie* GoldenEye.

SETI@home is a project that combines the resources of millions of people around the world, who use their personal computers to analyze small amounts of radio data. A special program provided by the project downloads a batch of data, analyzes it, and automatically transmits the results back to project headquarters in Berkeley, California. Imagine—if you join this project, you could be the one to pick up the message when E.T. calls!

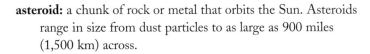

Glossary

asteroid: a chunk of rock or metal that orbits the Sun. Asteroids range in size from dust particles to as large as 900 miles (1,500 km) across.

astronaut: a space pilot

astronomer: a scientist who studies the universe

atmosphere: a mixture of gases that covers the surface of a planet or star

atoms: submicroscopic particles that are the basic building blocks of the chemical elements

axis: an imaginary line through the center of a sphere, around which it rotates

big bang theory: a belief that the universe began when a hot, dense mass of matter exploded and is still expanding from the force of that explosion

black hole: a dark region of space caused by the collapse of a massive star. The gravitational pull of the black hole is so strong, it sucks in anything that gets too close to it, including light.

comet: a small object made of snow, dust, and ice that orbits the Sun and has a streaking tail

constellation: a group of stars linked together mentally to form the outlines of people, animals, and objects

corona: the Sun's hot outer atmosphere. A corona appears as a halo during a total solar eclipse.

cosmonaut: a Russian space pilot

crater: a round, cup-shaped depression on a planet or moon, caused by a meteorite impact

dark matter: matter that cannot be detected directly but is believed to exist

Doppler effect: a shifting of the radiation given off by a moving object toward shorter or longer wavelengths, depending on the direction of movement. Doppler effects on light rays produce red shifts (objects moving away) and blue shifts (objects moving toward the observer).

ecliptic: an imaginary line along which the Sun appears to be moving across the sky

electromagnetic radiation: waves of energy that travel through space at the speed of light, which is 186,000 miles (nearly 300,000 km) per second

electromagnetic spectrum: a whole range of electromagnetic radiation that includes radio waves (longest wavelengths), microwaves, infrared, visible light, ultraviolet light, X-rays, and gamma rays (shortest wavelengths)

electromagnetic waves: waves consisting of electrical and magnetic fields traveling together

equator: the imaginary line that goes around the middle of Earth

evolution: the development of living organisms over a long period of time

fusion reaction: joining of the nuclei of light atoms to form the nucleus of a heavier atom, releasing enormous amounts of energy

galaxy: a large collection of stars held together by gravitational forces

gamma radiation: a very high-energy form of electromagnetic radiation released from the nuclei of atoms

gravity: a force of attraction between two objects; the attractive force that holds objects to Earth's surface

Kuiper belt (*pronounced* KYE-per): a region of space beyond Neptune, containing thousands of small ice/rock bodies in orbit around the Sun

light-year: the distance light travels in one year—186,000 miles (nearly 300,000 km) per second

lunar eclipse: a darkening of the Moon when it passes into Earth's shadow, preventing it from reflecting sunlight

magnetic field: the region of space near a magnet or current-carrying body in which magnetic forces, attracting or repelling objects, may be felt

meteor: a streak of light in the sky (also called a shooting star), caused by a small meteoroid burning up as it passes through Earth's atmosphere

meteorite: a meteoroid that falls to the surface of a planet or a moon, producing a crater

meteoroid: a piece of rock or dust from asteroids and comets found in space

nebula: a cloud of dust and gas in space; the birthplace of new stars or the remains of dying stars

nuclear fusion: the combining of nuclei (centers) of atoms to form heavier ones, releasing large amounts of energy in the process; the energy source for the stars

orbit: the curved path of one object that travels around a larger, more massive object

photosphere: a star's surface

prism: an angled piece of glass that splits light into the spectrum of colors

pulsar: a spinning neutron star that emits radio waves at regular intervals

quasar: a very bright center of a very distant galaxy; the most distant object ever observed

radio telescope: a telescope that uses radio waves to form images

revolution: the movement of one body around another in an orbit, such as the planets orbiting the Sun

rotation: turning around on an axis

satellite: any object in space that orbits a larger object, including moons and artificial satellites in orbit around planets

solar eclipse: darkening of the Sun that occurs when the Moon passes between the Sun and Earth, blocking the Sun's light

solar flare: an explosive release of hot gases from the Sun's surface

solar system: the Sun together with planets, asteroids, and other bodies that revolve around the Sun

solar wind: hot, electrically charged gas particles that constantly escape from the Sun's surface and fly out into space

spectroscope: an instrument that breaks down light or other electromagnetic radiation into its spectrum; also called a spectrograph

spectrum: the band of colors produced by the separation of light of different wavelengths

sunspots: dark spots that appear on the surface of the Sun from time to time, in areas where magnetic fields keep hot gases from rising

supernova: the explosion of an extremely large star

Van Allen belt: doughnut-shaped bands of intense radiation consisting of charged particles trapped by the magnetic fields that surround Earth

visible light: the part of the electromagnetic spectrum that humans can see

wavelength: the distance between the top of one wave and the top of another

Selected Bibliography

Books

Becklake, Sue. *All about Space*. New York: Scholastic, 1998.

Couper, Heather, and Nigel Henbest. *Big Bang*. New York: Dorling Kindersley, 1997.

———. *Space Encyclopedia*. New York: Dorling Kindersley, 1999.

Hawkes, Nigel. *Mysteries of the Universe*. Brookfield, CT: Copper Beech Books, 2000.

Lippincott, Kristen. *Astronomy*. New York: Dorling Kindersley, 1999.

Miller, Ron. *Extrasolar Planets*. Minneapolis: Twenty-First Century Books, 2002.

———. *The Sun*. Minneapolis: Twenty-First Century Books, 2002.

Simon, Seymour. *The Universe*. New York: HarperCollins Publishers, 1998.

Time-Life Education. *The Universe*. Alexandria, VA: Time-Life Books, 1998.

Articles

Adler, Jerry. "Of Cosmic Proportions: Astronomers Decide Pluto Isn't a Real Planet Anymore. Why They Did It—and How Our View of the Universe Is Changing." *Newsweek*, September 4, 2006, 44–50.

Courtland, Rachel. "Phoenix Finds Evidence of Past Liquid Water on Mars." *New Scientist Space*. September 29, 2008. http://space.newscientist.com/article/dn14837-phoenix-finds-evidence-of-past-liquid-water-on-mars.html (October 12, 2008).

Fisher, Diane. "Inventions from Space." *The Space Place.* September 8, 2005. http://spaceplace.nasa.gov/en/kids/spinoffs2.shtml (May 30, 2008).

Hillebrandt, Wolfgang, Hans-Thomas Janka, and Ewald Muller. "How to Blow Up a Star." *Scientific American*, October 2006, 43–49.

Phillips, Tony. "Jupiter's New Red Spot." *NASA.* March 3, 2006. http://science.nasa.gov/headlines/y2006/02mar_redjr.htm (June 2, 2008).

Piazza, Enrico. "Cassini-Huygens: Mission to Saturn and Titan." *NASA.* January 10, 2008. http://saturn.jpl.nasa.gov/overview/index.cfm (June 8, 2008).

Than, Ker. "Major Discovery: New Planet Could Harbor Water and Life." *SPACE.com.* April 24, 2007. http://www.space.com/scienceastronomy/070424_hab_exoplanet.html (February 15, 2008).

Tobin, Kate. "Mars Lander Sends Photos from Red Planet's Arctic." *CNN.com.* May 26, 2008. http://www.cnn.com/2008/TECH/space/05/26/mars.lander/index.html?eref=rss_topstories#cnnSTCText (May 26, 2008).

Vakoch, Douglas. "Setting SETI's Sights: Latest Planet Discovery Suggests New Targets." *SPACE.com.* June 16, 2005. http://www.space.com/searchforlife/seti_newplanet-050616.html (May 30, 2008).

Webster, Guy, and Dwayne Brown. "NASA Extends Operations for Its Long-Lived Mars Rovers." *Mars Exploration Rover Mission: Press Releases, NASA.* October 15, 2007. http://marsrovers.jpl.nasa/pressreleases/20071015a.html (June 5, 2008).

Webster, Guy, Erica Hupp, and Dwayne Brown. "NASA Images Suggest Water Still Flows in Brief Spurts on Mars." *NASA.* December 6, 2006. http://www.nasa.gov/mission_pages/mars/news/mgs-20061206.html (June 2, 2008).

Whitlock, Laura. "Van Allen Belts and Spacecraft." *Ask an Astrophysicist.* June 30, 1997. http://imagine.gsfc.nasa.gov/docs/ask_astro/answers/970630a.html (June 2, 2008).

Young, Kelly. "Pluto Probe Begins Close-up Study of Jupiter." *New Scientist*. January 8, 2007. http://space.newscientist .com/article/dn10923-pluto-probe-begins-closeup-study- of-jupiter.html (June 5, 2008).

Videos

Eyewitness—Planets. London: Dorling Kindersley, 1997.

Nova: Runaway Universe. Boston: WGBH—Boston Video, 2000.

The Universe: An Amazing Journey from the Sun to the Most Distant Galaxies. Washougal, WA: Universe Productions, 2003.

The Universe—The Complete Season One. New York: A&E Home Video, 2007.

The Universe—The Complete Season Two. New York: A&E Home Video, 2008.

For Further Information

Books

Conway, Andrew, and Rosie Coleman. *A Beginner's Guide to the Universe.* Cambridge: Cambridge University Press, 2003.

Dinwiddie, Robert, Philip Eales, David Hughes, Ian Nicholson, Ian Ridpath, Giles Sparrow, Pam Spence, Carole Stott, Kevin Tildsley, and Martin Rees. *Universe.* New York: DK Publishing, 2005.

Dowswell, Paul. *The Usborne First Encyclopedia of Space.* London: Usborne Publishing, 2001.

Fleisher, Paul. *The Big Bang.* Minneapolis: Twenty-First Century Books, 2006.

Sasaki, Chris. *The Constellations: Stars & Stories.* New York: Sterling Publishing, 2003.

Scott, Elaine. *When Is a Planet Not a Planet: The Story of Pluto.* New York: Clarion Books, 2007.

Vogt, Gregory L. *Earth's Outer Atmosphere: Bordering Space.* Minneapolis: Twenty-First Century Books, 2007.

Woods, Michael, and Mary B. Woods. *Space Disasters.* Minneapolis: Lerner Publications Company, 2008.

Websites

Amazing Space
http://amazing-space.stsci.edu/
This site has interactive activities about stars, comets, black holes, and telescopes. It also features movies, games, and a guide to constellations with highlights of sky watching for the current month.

ESA Kids: Life in Space
http://www.esa.int/esaKIDSen/LifeinSpace.html
This is a lively website with photos, videos, and articles on astronauts, space stations, living in space, exploration, and the possibility of life on other planets. Interactive puzzles, quizzes, and instructions for building models add to the fun.

KidsAstronomy.com

http://www.kidsastronomy.com/

This kid-friendly site has information, games, and activities about the solar system and space exploration. You can also play educational songs, look up words in an astronomy dictionary, download free computer wallpaper, and take free online classes.

NASA Kids' Club

http://www.nasa.gov/audience/forkids/kidsclub/flash/index .html

This kid-friendly site offers interactive games at five skill levels. Check terms in a picture dictionary and sign up to send your name to the Moon.

NASA Science

http://nasascience.nasa.gov/

This site has articles, spectacular photos, and news items about Earth, the Sun, the solar system, space exploration and the universe, plus a special "NASA Science for Kids" fun site with games, activities, and art.

The Planetary Society

http://www.planetary.org/

This site has articles, news, and photos on space explorations and the projects of "the world's largest space interest group, . . . dedicated to inspiring the public with the adventure and mystery of space exploration."

SETI@home Needs Your Help

http://setiathome.berkeley.edu/

This site tells you how SETI@home works, with a link for signing up to participate in computer processing of radio data from outer space.

Space.com
>http://www.space.com/
>Check this site for articles about the universe and space exploration with space images. Watch NASA TV live.

U.S. Space & Rocket Center
>http://www.spacecamp.com/
>This site gives details about the Davidson Center for Space Exploration, a museum with rockets, spaceflight hardware, and interactive exhibits and spaceflight simulators. You can sign up for three- and six-day space camp programs for kids (ages 9–11, 12–14, 15–18) and for adults.

Index

Photo Acknowledgments

The images in this book are used with the permission of: © Kim Westerskov/Stone/ Getty Images, p. 5; © Antonio M. Rosario/The Image Bank/Getty Images, p. 7; NASA/JSC, pp. 9, 16 (third from top, left), 32 (third from top), 75 (both), 76, 77, 81 (top), 87; © age fotostock/SuperStock, pp. 10, 14, 34; © Jean-Leon Huens/National Geographic/Getty Images, p. 11 (top); © Mansell/Time & Life Pictures/Getty Images, p. 11 (bottom); © Italian School/The Bridgeman Art Library/Getty Images, p. 12; © Laura Westlund/Independent Picture Service, pp. 15, 16 (diagram), 21, 28, 31, 52, 57; NASA/Johns Hopkins University Applied Physics Laboratory/Carnegie Institution of Washington, pp. 16 (top), 32 (top); © SuperStock, Inc./SuperStock, pp. 16 (second from top), 32 (second from top); NASA/JPL/USGS, pp. 16 (third from top, right; second from bottom), 32 (second from bottom), 35; NASA/JPL/MSSS, pp. 16 (fourth from top), 32 (fourth from top), 38; NASA/JPL, pp. 16 (fourth from bottom, bottom), 29, 32 (fourth from bottom, bottom), 40, 41, 43 (both); NASA and The Hubble Heritage Team (STScI/AURA), pp. 16 (third from bottom), 32 (third from bottom); NASA/JPL-Caltech, pp. 18, 45, 68; ESA/NASA/SOHO, p. 20; Photo by Solar and Heliospheric Observatory (SOHO) via Getty Images, p. 22; © Digital Vision/Getty Images, p. 23; © CORBIS, p. 24; © The Copyright Group/SuperStock, p. 27; © Pacific Stock/SuperStock, p. 36; NASA/JPL-Caltech/University of Arizona, p. 39; © Claus Lunau/Bonnier Publications/Photo Researchers, Inc., p. 46; © Chad Baker/Photodisc/Getty Images, p. 48 (top); © Travel Ink/Gallo Images/Getty Images, p. 48 (bottom); © Space Frontiers/Hulton Archive/Getty Images, p. 50; © Yoshinori Watabe/Amana Images/Getty Images, p. 53; © Ernest Manewal/SuperStock, p. 55; NASA, ESA and The Hubble Heritage Team (STScI/AURA), p. 62; AP Photo, pp. 65, 74; NASA, ESA, C. Heymans (University of British Columbia, Vancouver), M. Gray (University of Nottingham, U.K.), M. Barden (Innsbruck), the STAGES collaboration, C. Wolf (Oxford University, U.K.), K. Meisenheimer (Max-Planck Institute for Astronomy, Heidelberg), and the COMBO-17 collaboration, p. 66; NASA, ESA, and A. Nota (STScI/ESA), p. 69; © Ken Graham/Stone/Getty Images, p. 71; AP Photo/TASS, p. 73; NASA/KSC, p. 81 (bottom); NASA/JPL-Caltech/Cornell, p. 83; NASA/JPL-Caltech/University of Arizona/Texas A&M, p. 84; © Erik Simonsen/Photographer's Choice/Getty Images, p. 92; © Louie Psihoyos/Science Faction/Getty Images, p. 94; © GeoEye/Photo Researchers, Inc., p. 96 (top); © StockTrek/Photodisc/Getty Images, p. 96 (bottom);

Front Cover: NASA, ESA, and the Hubble Heritage (STScI/AURA)-ESA/Hubble Collaboration, Acknowledgment: J. Maíz Apellániz (Institute of Astrophysics of Andalucía, Spain).

About the Authors

Dr. Alvin Silverstein is a former professor of Biology and director of the Physician Assistant Program at the College of Staten Island of the City University of New York. Virginia B. Silverstein is a translator of Russian scientific literature.

The Silversteins' collaboration began with a biochemical research project at the University of Pennsylvania. Since then they have produced six children and more than two hundred published books that have received high acclaim for their clear, timely, and authoritative coverage of science and health topics.

Laura Silverstein Nunn, a graduate of Kean College, began helping with the research for her parents' books while she was in high school. Since joining the writing team, she has coauthored more than eighty books.